U.S.A. TRAVEL GUIDES

ALABAMA

BY ANN HEINRICHS • ILLUSTRATED BY MATT KANIA

The Child's World®

childsworld.com

Published by The Child's World®
1980 Lookout Drive • Mankato, MN 56003-1705
800-599-READ • www.childsworld.com

Printing

Printed in the United States of America
PA02334

Ann Heinrichs is the author of more than 100 books for children and young adults. She has also enjoyed successful careers as a children's book editor and an advertising copywriter. Ann grew up in Fort Smith, Arkansas, and lives in Chicago, Illinois.

About the Author
Ann Heinrichs

Matt Kania loves maps and, as a kid, dreamed of making them. In school he studied geography and cartography, and today he makes maps for a living. Matt's favorite thing about drawing maps is learning about the places they represent. Many of the maps he has created can be found in books, magazines, videos, Web sites, and public places.

About the
Map Illustrator
Matt Kania

*On the cover: Walk up the steps to the state capitol
in Montgomery and see how laws are made.*

OUR ALABAMA TRIP

ALABAMA

Hey! How about a tour through the Heart of Dixie? That's Alabama! You'll climb Goat Hill. You'll learn about a coon dog named Troop. You'll hike past waterfalls and take space rides. You'll even see Moon Pies flying through the air! Just follow that loopy dotted line. Or make your own trip by skipping around. Ready? Then buckle up. We're off!

WELCOME TO
ALABAMA

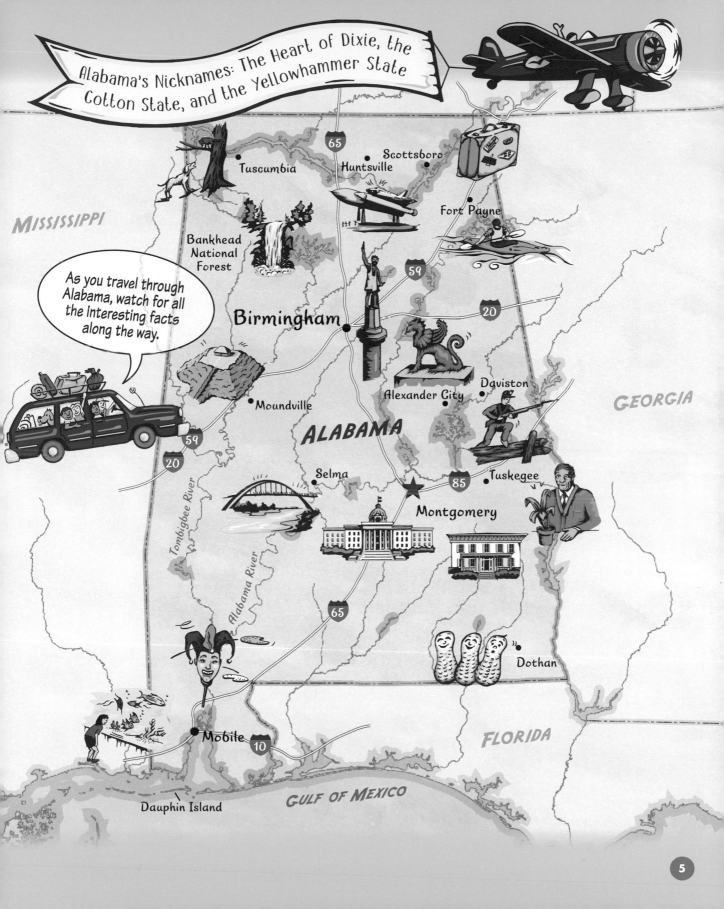

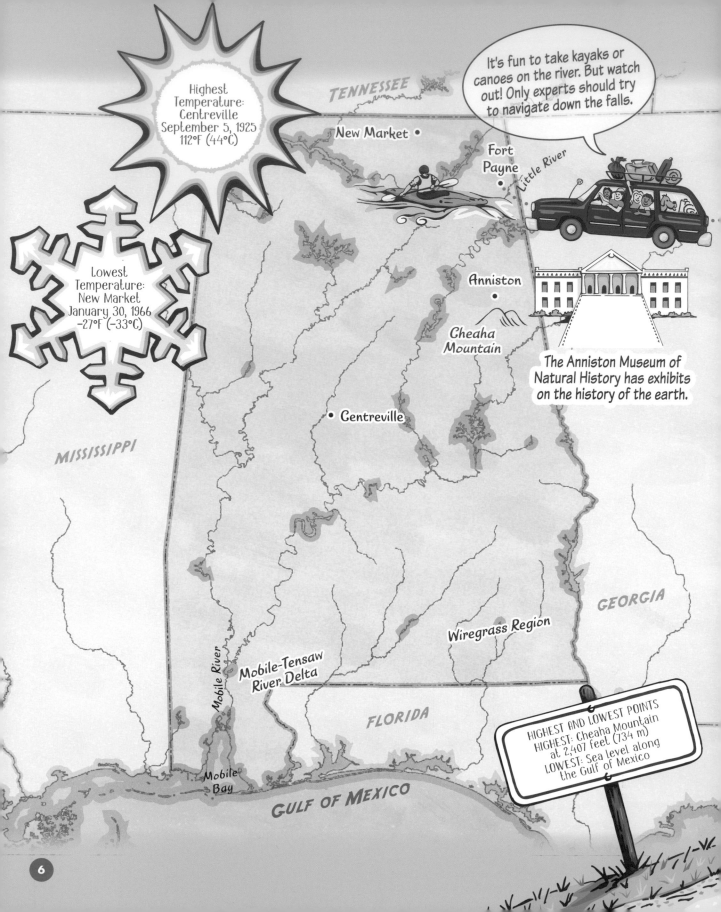

KAYAKING IN LITTLE RIVER CANYON

Whee! The **kayak** plunges down the waterfall. Foamy spray is splashing everywhere. What a blast! It's the thundering waterfall in Little River **Canyon** near Fort Payne.

The Little River is in northeastern Alabama. Mountains and hills cover much of the northeast. Rivers cut deep valleys through them.

The rest of Alabama is lower and more level. The southeast is called the Wiregrass Region. Really tough grass used to grow there. Now it's a rich farming area.

The Mobile-Tensaw River **Delta** is in the southwest. It has many swamps and **bayous**. The river empties into Mobile Bay. That's part of the Gulf of Mexico. Lots of sandy beaches lie along the coast.

Kayakers love Little River Falls. You can see awesome kayaking action there.

DAUPHIN ISLAND SEA LAB ESTUARIUM

I t's cool. It's wet. It's got a shell and a long tail. And you're holding it in your hands! Eek!

You're at the Dauphin Island Sea Lab Estuarium. You're handling critters in the touch tank. Can you guess what this one is? It's a horseshoe crab!

Dauphin Island is in the Gulf of Mexico. Sea turtles and crabs live around there. Whales and sharks swim out in the gulf.

Alabama is famous for its flowers. Mobile likes to show off its colorful azaleas. Thick pine forests cover much of Alabama. There you'll find bobcats, foxes, rabbits, and deer. Alligators live in the southern swamps.

Ghost crabs bury themselves in sand to keep cool during the day.

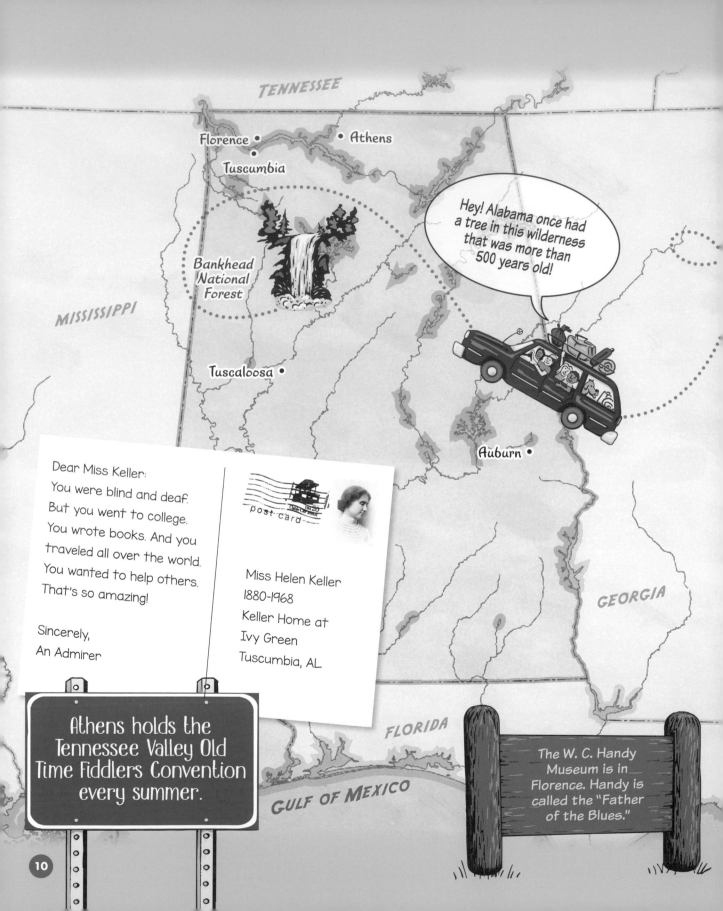

TENNESSEE

Florence •
• Athens
Tuscumbia •

Bankhead National Forest

MISSISSIPPI

Tuscaloosa •

Hey! Alabama once had a tree in this wilderness that was more than 500 years old!

Auburn •

GEORGIA

Dear Miss Keller:
You were blind and deaf. But you went to college. You wrote books. And you traveled all over the world. You wanted to help others. That's so amazing!

Sincerely,
An Admirer

post card

Miss Helen Keller
1880-1968
Keller Home at
Ivy Green
Tuscumbia, AL

FLORIDA

Athens holds the Tennessee Valley Old Time Fiddlers Convention every summer.

GULF OF MEXICO

The W. C. Handy Museum is in Florence. Handy is called the "Father of the Blues."

Let's see. Three hundred one, three hundred two . . . . You're deep in the Sipsey Wilderness Area. It's in Bankhead National Forest. It's called the land of a thousand waterfalls. But don't try to count them. It's more fun to go hiking!

There's a lot to see and do in Alabama. Some people explore the mountains and forests. Others enjoy museums, music festivals, or sports.

Football is big in Alabama. The Crimson Tide is a popular team. It's from the University of Alabama in Tuscaloosa. Auburn University's Tigers are popular, too.

Sipsey Wilderness Area is the largest wilderness in the state. Dip your feet into the relaxing water!

INDIAN SUMMER DAY CAMP AT MOUNDVILLE

Cut that **gourd** in two. Now, how about making a mask? Cut out eyes and a mouth. Then get some paint and have fun! Red for the eyes. Yellow for the nose. How about blue for the mouth? You're at Indian Summer Day Camp at Moundville!

Native Americans once lived at Moundville. Their city covered hundreds of acres. They built many huge mounds of earth. Some mounds had the leaders' homes on top. Other mounds were graves. The people made pottery and stone and copper goods. Want to learn more about them? Just check out Moundville's museum, classes, and camps.

The mounds at Moundville are huge! Try and imagine what life was like living here.

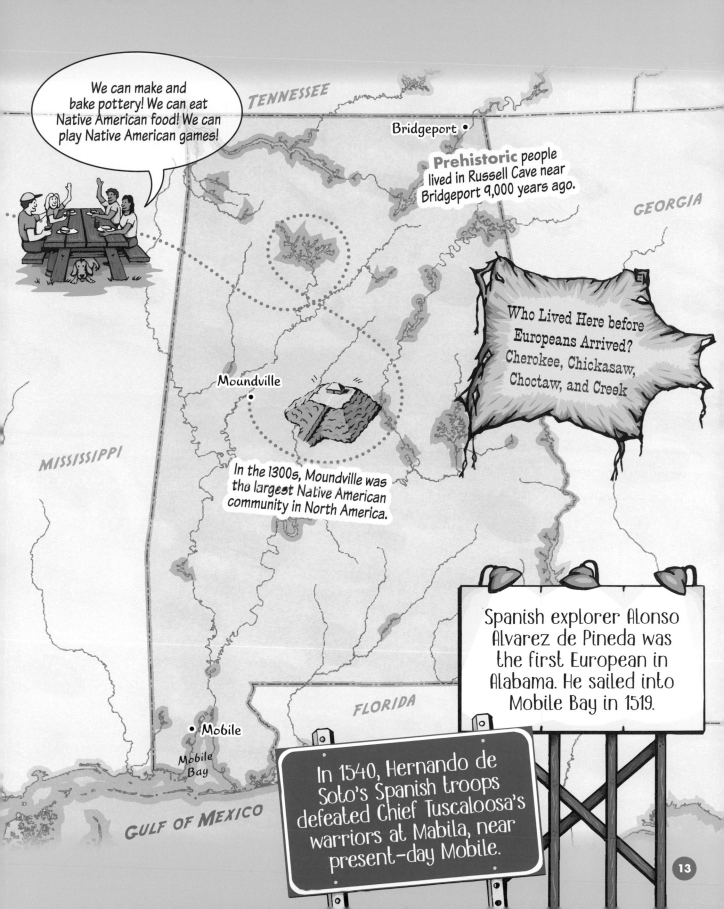

We can make and bake pottery! We can eat Native American food! We can play Native American games!

TENNESSEE

Bridgeport

Prehistoric people lived in Russell Cave near Bridgeport 9,000 years ago.

GEORGIA

Who Lived Here before Europeans Arrived? Cherokee, Chickasaw, Choctaw, and Creek

Moundville

In the 1300s, Moundville was the largest Native American community in North America.

MISSISSIPPI

Spanish explorer Alonso Alvarez de Pineda was the first European in Alabama. He sailed into Mobile Bay in 1519.

FLORIDA

Mobile

Mobile Bay

In 1540, Hernando de Soto's Spanish troops defeated Chief Tuscaloosa's warriors at Mabila, near present-day Mobile.

GULF OF MEXICO

13

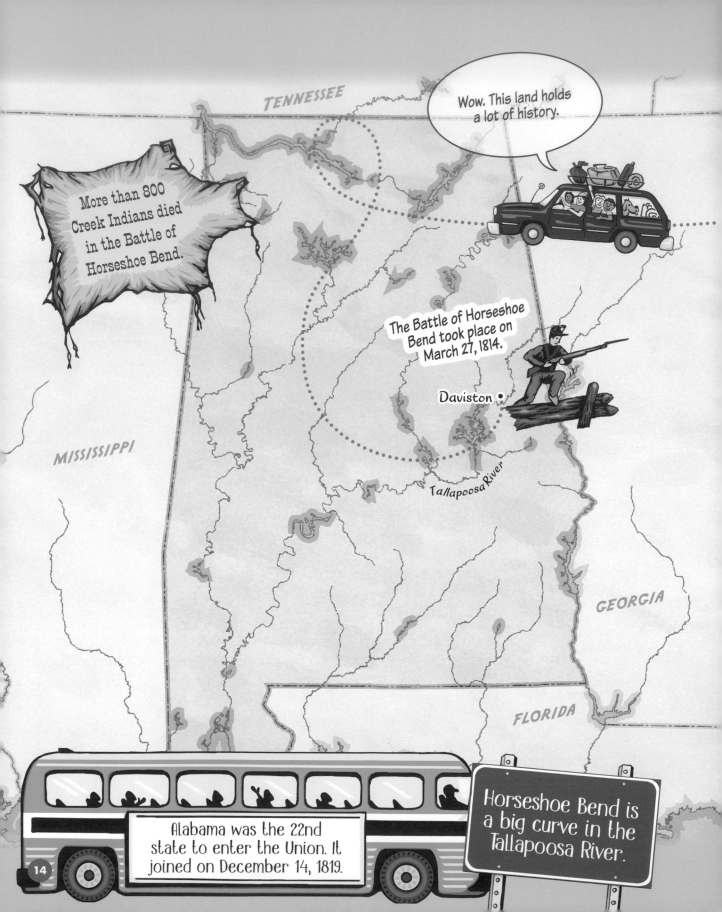

HORSESHOE BEND NATIONAL MILITARY PARK

Stand up straight! Chin down, shoulders back! It's 1814. You're a soldier under Andrew Jackson. And you're lined up for a drill. No slouching!

Actually, you're in a program at Horseshoe Bend near Daviston. General Jackson defeated the Creek Indians here. The Creeks were forced to give up their homeland. It included more than half of present-day Alabama.

Spanish explorers arrived in Alabama in the 1500s. Then white settlers moved in. Little by little, the Native Americans were pushed out. This continued throughout the early 19th century. The Creek Indians continued to be forced, tricked, and cheated out of their land. Thousands had leave the land that their families had occupied for generations.

The Battle of Horseshoe Bend ended the Creek War. The Creek Indians lost all their land in the war.

THE FIRST WHITE HOUSE OF THE CONFEDERACY

FIRST WHITE HOUSE OF THE CONFEDERACY

Designated Executive Residence by the Provisional Confederate Congress February 21, 1861. President Jefferson Davis and his family lived here until the Confederate Capital moved to Richmond summer 1861. Built by William Sayre 1832-35 at Bibb and Lee Streets. Moved to present location by the First White House Association and dedicated June 3, 1921.

Okay. It's white. And it's a house. Does that make it the White House? Well, sort of. It's the First White House of the Confederacy. It stands in Montgomery, the first capital of the Confederacy.

The Confederacy was made up of several Southern states. They formed their own nation in 1861. The Confederacy fought the Union, or Northern states, over slavery. This was called the Civil War (1861–1865).

Much of the South depended on farming. In Alabama, farmers grew cotton on large farms. African American slaves were forced to work on these farms. Most Northerners opposed slavery. In the end, the North won. Then the slaves were freed. It was a long way to equality, however.

There's a White House in Alabama? Learn about the Confederacy as you tour it.

TENNESSEE

Dixie is a nickname for the South. That's why Alabama is called the Heart of Dixie.

Quiz time: Who lives in the White House in Washington, DC? Answer: The U.S. president.

GEORGIA

Montgomery ★

Eleven states made up the Confederacy, or Confederate States of America. They were Alabama, Arkansas, Florida, Georgia, Louisiana, Mississippi, North Carolina, South Carolina, Tennessee, Texas, and Virginia.

MISSISSIPPI

Alabama's largest Civil War battle was the 1864 Battle of Mobile Bay. Union forces won.

FLORIDA

Mobile Bay

GULF OF MEXICO

Jefferson Davis was the Confederate president. He lived in the Confederacy's White House.

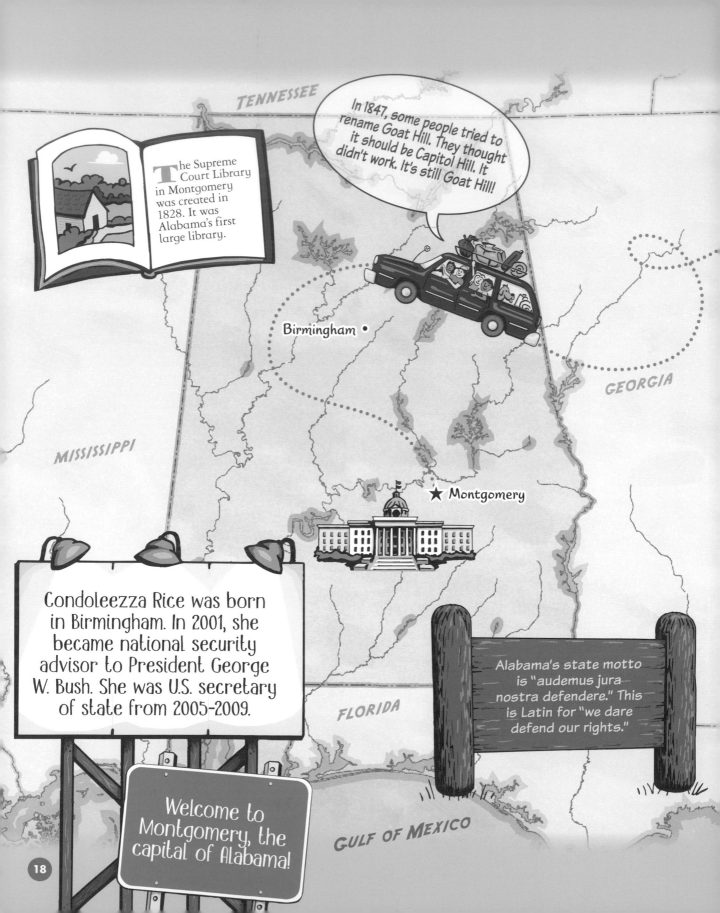

The Supreme Court Library in Montgomery was created in 1828. It was Alabama's first large library.

In 1847, some people tried to rename Goat Hill. They thought it should be Capitol Hill. It didn't work. It's still Goat Hill!

TENNESSEE

MISSISSIPPI

Birmingham •

GEORGIA

★ Montgomery

Condoleezza Rice was born in Birmingham. In 2001, she became national security advisor to President George W. Bush. She was U.S. secretary of state from 2005-2009.

Alabama's state motto is "audemus jura nostra defendere." This is Latin for "we dare defend our rights."

FLORIDA

Welcome to Montgomery, the capital of Alabama!

GULF OF MEXICO

THE STATE CAPITOL ON GOAT HILL

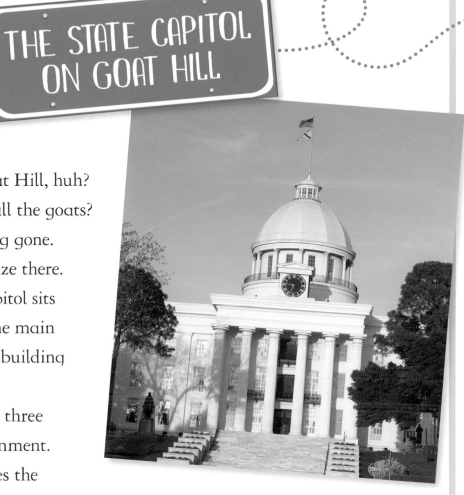

So this is Goat Hill, huh? Where are all the goats? Sorry! They're long gone. Goats used to graze there. Now the state capitol sits on that hill. It's the main state government building in Montgomery.

Alabama has three branches of government. One branch makes the state's laws. It's called the legislature. The governor heads another branch. It is called the executive branch. It carries out the laws. Judges make up the third branch. They decide whether someone has broken a law.

So this is where Alabama's laws are made. Imagine all those busy government workers inside!

BIRMINGHAM'S VULCAN STATUE

Hmm. His ears aren't pointy. He doesn't wear a *Star Trek* outfit. And he doesn't say, "Live long and prosper." Is this guy really a Vulcan? He sure is. He's Vulcan himself!

For ancient Romans, Vulcan was the god of fire. They believed he made metals with the fire. So what's his statue doing in Birmingham?

Alabama is home to many valuable minerals. One is iron. Birmingham began making iron into steel in the 1880s. Fiery furnaces melted the metals. Alabama became a leader in iron and steel. Vulcan stands for these industries. He's got a hammer and a spear point—but no pointy ears!

The Vulcan is 56 feet (17 m) tall. He weighs 101,200 pounds (45,904 kg).

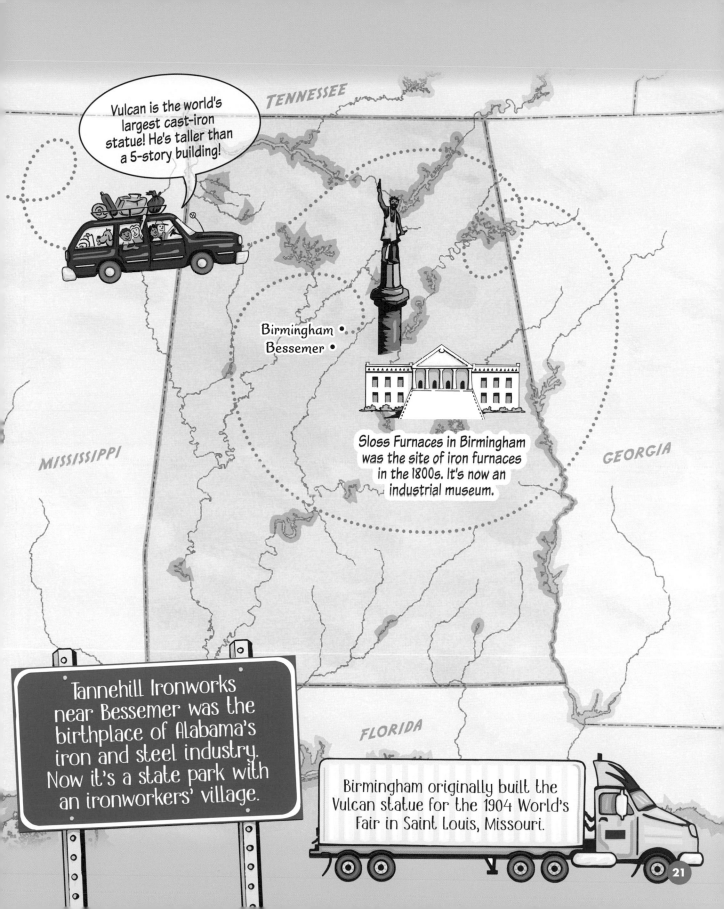

Vulcan is the world's largest cast-iron statue! He's taller than a 5-story building!

TENNESSEE

MISSISSIPPI

Birmingham •
Bessemer •

Sloss Furnaces in Birmingham was the site of iron furnaces in the 1800s. It's now an industrial museum.

GEORGIA

FLORIDA

Tannehill Ironworks near Bessemer was the birthplace of Alabama's iron and steel industry. Now it's a state park with an ironworkers' village.

Birmingham originally built the Vulcan statue for the 1904 World's Fair in Saint Louis, Missouri.

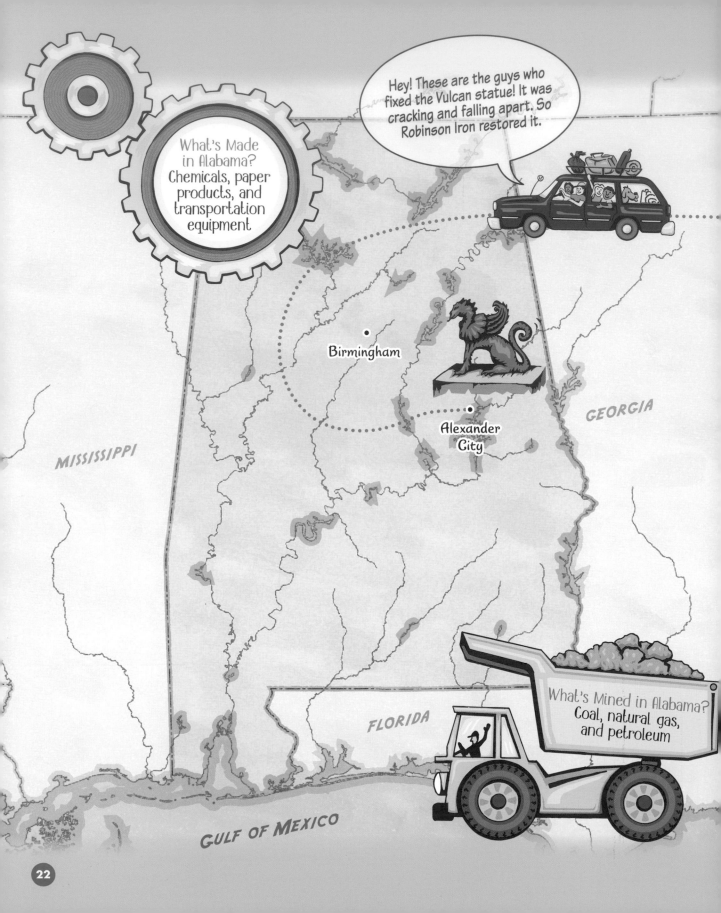

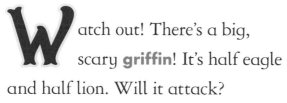

ROBINSON IRON IN ALEXANDER CITY

Watch out! There's a big, scary **griffin**! It's half eagle and half lion. Will it attack?

Not this one. You're on a factory tour of Robinson Iron. Workers there make all kinds of iron products. They make fountains, fences, and parts of buildings. And big, scary griffins, too!

Alabama has many busy factories. They make everything from airplane engines to paper bags. Want another fun tour? Visit the Golden Flake snack foods factory in Birmingham. Yum!

Robinson Iron has done work for many famous buildings. They even restore fountains!

GEORGE WASHINGTON CARVER'S LAB AT TUSKEGEE INSTITUTE

Microscopes, burners, grinders, and scales. Is this a mad scientist's lab? Nope. It's George Washington Carver's lab at Tuskegee Institute in Tuskegee.

Carver was an African American scientist. He had lots of great ideas. He developed better ways to farm. Carver also worked with peanuts and sweet potatoes. He developed hundreds of new products with them.

Booker T. Washington helped found Tuskegee Institute in 1881. The school was created to train African American teachers. Washington hired Carver and many other fine professors. Today, the school is called Tuskegee University.

Imagine lunches without peanut butter! Thanks, George Washington Carver.

So what'll it be? Creamy, crunchy, or extra crunchy? Only one wins the peanut butter grand prize! You're at Dothan's National Peanut Festival. It's the largest peanut festival in the world!

Peanuts are a big deal in the Dothan area. About half the nation's peanuts grow there. But cotton is Alabama's most valuable crop. People called it King Cotton in the 1800s. That's because it ruled the state's **economy**. Now chickens and cattle are the leading farm products. They bring in much more income than cotton.

Alabamans catch shrimp, crabs, and fish, too. Ever heard of a fish farm? Some farmers raise catfish in big ponds.

Alabama still grows lots of cotton.

SELMA'S NATIONAL VOTING RIGHTS MUSEUM

She was just 11 years old. Police on horseback were everywhere. **Tear gas** was burning her eyes. Soon she was thrown in jail. What's going on here?

The year is 1965. The girl is Joanne Bland. She and others were gathered in Selma. They planned to march to Montgomery. They wanted voting rights for African Americans. They hoped Montgomery's lawmakers would support their cause. The Voting Rights Act was passed later that year.

You'll get the whole story in Selma. Just stop by the National Voting Rights Museum. And guess what? Joanne became one of the museum's directors!

Many people fought for civil rights in Alabama. Learn about their work in Selma.

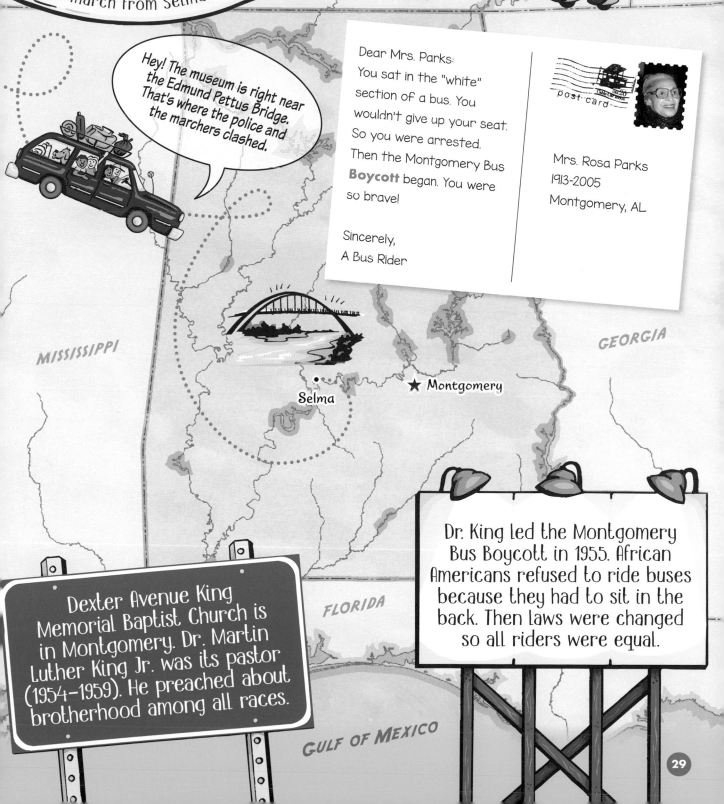

Thousands of people joined the **civil rights** march from Selma to Montgomery in 1965.

Hey! The museum is right near the Edmund Pettus Bridge. That's where the police and the marchers clashed.

Dear Mrs. Parks:
You sat in the "white" section of a bus. You wouldn't give up your seat. So you were arrested. Then the Montgomery Bus **Boycott** began. You were so brave!

Sincerely,
A Bus Rider

post card

Mrs. Rosa Parks
1913-2005
Montgomery, AL

MISSISSIPPI

GEORGIA

Selma

★ Montgomery

Dr. King led the Montgomery Bus Boycott in 1955. African Americans refused to ride buses because they had to sit in the back. Then laws were changed so all riders were equal.

Dexter Avenue King Memorial Baptist Church is in Montgomery. Dr. Martin Luther King Jr. was its pastor (1954–1959). He preached about brotherhood among all races.

FLORIDA

GULF OF MEXICO

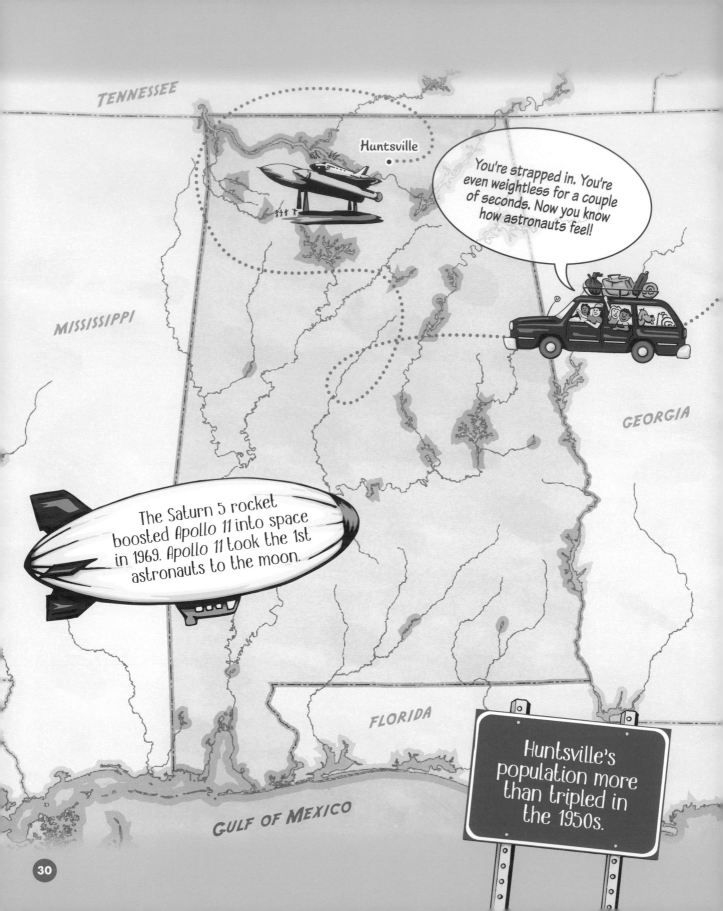

THE U.S. SPACE AND ROCKET CENTER IN HUNTSVILLE

Five, four, three, two, one, liftoff! You shoot up 14 stories in just a few seconds. Then you freefall straight down. You're at the U.S. Space and Rocket Center in Huntsville. And you're trying out the wild space rides!

Huntsville is called Rocket City, U.S.A. Space scientists started working there in 1950. They developed many spacecraft. Their rockets helped send astronauts to the moon. Huntsville is still an important space center.

Feel like learning about things out of this world? You can attend space camp here!

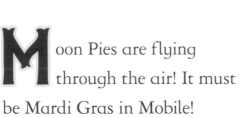

MARDI GRAS IN MOBILE

Moon Pies are flying through the air! It must be Mardi Gras in Mobile!

Mardi Gras is a big carnival. In Mobile, the fun lasts for two whole weeks. People celebrate with costumes and colorful parades. People toss beads from the parade floats. And some toss Moon Pies, too!

Alabamans have roots all over the world. Just look at Huntsville. More than 100 languages are spoken there!

Mobile held America's first Mardi Gras in 1703. People still celebrate all over the country!

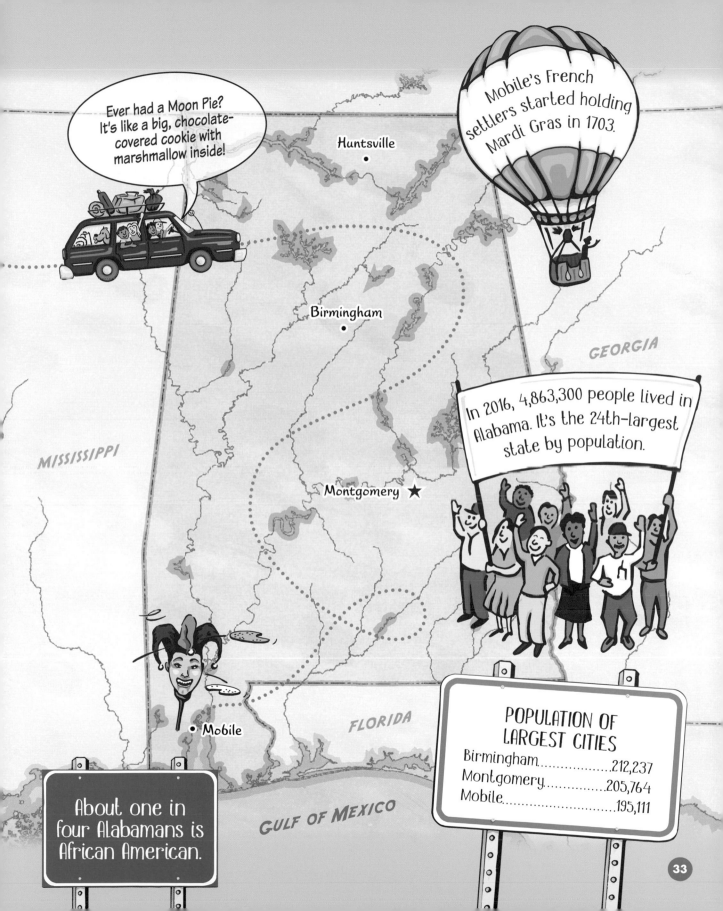

TENNESSEE

• Tuscumbia

Troop's owner, Key Underwood, buried him on September 4, 1937.

Aww! People even put flowers on the graves. There's Night Ranger and Patches and Smoky . . .

MISSISSIPPI

GEORGIA

Not just any coon dog can get in the cemetery. Owners have to prove their dog was a skilled hunter.

FLORIDA

On Labor Day in September, coon hunters gather at the cemetery to honor the memory of their dogs.

GULF OF MEXICO

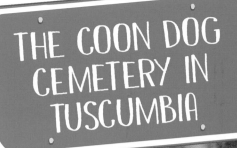

THE COON DOG CEMETERY IN TUSCUMBIA

He wasn't fluffy. He wasn't cute. But he sure could hunt. He was Troop, the coon dog. That's a dog that helps hunt raccoons.

Troop was the best coon dog ever. His owner thought so, anyhow. He buried Troop in a quiet, grassy place. Now that place is the Coon Dog Memorial Graveyard. It's in the little town of Tuscumbia. Almost 200 coon dogs rest there!

The cemetery was created in 1937, and it is only for coon dogs!

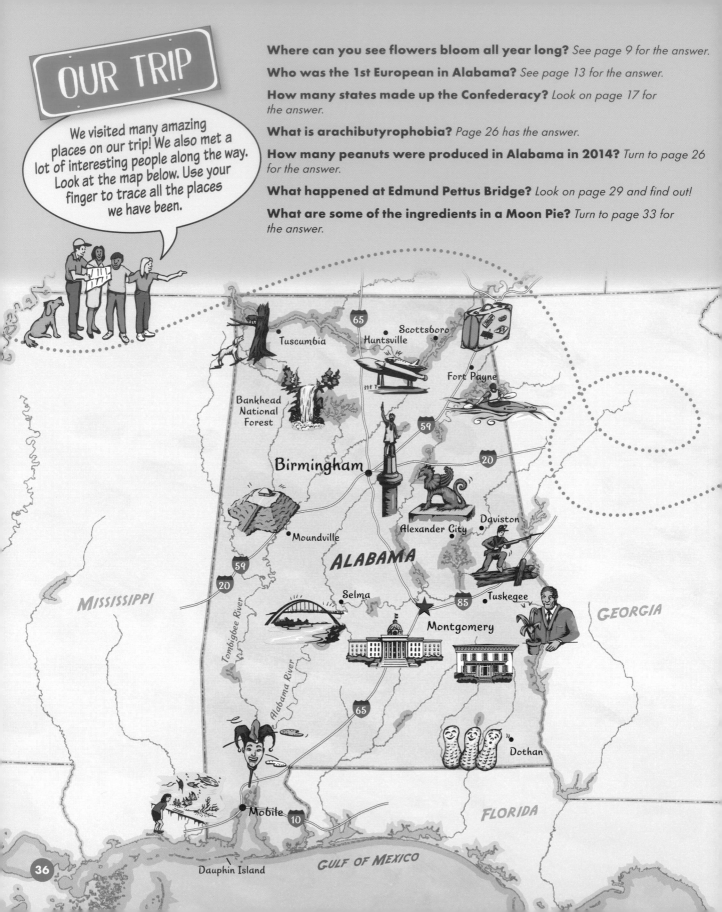

OUR TRIP

We visited many amazing places on our trip! We also met a lot of interesting people along the way. Look at the map below. Use your finger to trace all the places we have been.

Where can you see flowers bloom all year long? *See page 9 for the answer.*

Who was the 1st European in Alabama? *See page 13 for the answer.*

How many states made up the Confederacy? *Look on page 17 for the answer.*

What is arachibutyrophobia? *Page 26 has the answer.*

How many peanuts were produced in Alabama in 2014? *Turn to page 26 for the answer.*

What happened at Edmund Pettus Bridge? *Look on page 29 and find out!*

What are some of the ingredients in a Moon Pie? *Turn to page 33 for the answer.*

Tuscumbia

Scottsboro

Huntsville

Fort Payne

Bankhead National Forest

Birmingham

Daviston

Moundville

Alexander City

ALABAMA

Tuskegee

MISSISSIPPI

Tombigbee River

Alabama River

Selma

Montgomery

GEORGIA

Dothan

Mobile

FLORIDA

Dauphin Island

GULF OF MEXICO

STATE SYMBOLS

State American folk dance: Square dance

State amphibian: Red Hills salamander

State bird: Northern Flicker

State flower: Camellia

State fossil: *Basilosaurus cetoides* (zeuglodon)

State freshwater fish: Largemouth bass

State game bird: Wild turkey

State gemstone: Star blue quartz

State horse: Racking horse

State insect: Monarch butterfly

State mascot and butterfly:
Eastern tiger swallowtail

State mineral: Hematite (red iron ore)

State nut: Pecan

State reptile: Alabama red-bellied turtle

State rock: Marble

State saltwater fish: Fighting tarpon

State shell: *Scaphella junonia johnstonae* (Johnstone's junonia)

State soil: Bama soil series

State tree: Southern longleaf pine

State wildflower: Oak-leaf hydrangea

STATE SONG

"ALABAMA"

Words by Julia S. Tutwiler, music by Edna Gockel Gussen

From thy Southern shore where groweth,
By the sea thine orange tree.
To thy Northern vale where floweth
Deep and blue thy Tennessee.
Alabama, Alabama
We will aye be true to thee!

Broad the Stream whose name thou bearest;
Grand thy Bigbee rolls along;
Fair thy Coosa-Tallapoosa
Bold thy Warrior, dark and strong.
Goodlier than the land that Moses
Climbed lone Nebo's Mount to see
Alabama, Alabama,
We will aye be true to thee!

From thy prairies broad and fertile,
Where thy snow-white cotton shines.
To the hills where coal and iron
Hide in thy exhaustless mines.
Strong-armed miners—sturdy farmers:
Loyal hearts what'er we be.
Alabama, Alabama,
We will aye be true to thee!

From the quarries where the marble
White as that of Paros gleams

Waiting till thy sculptor's chisel,
Wake to like thy poet's dream;
For not only wealth of nature,
Wealth of mind hast thou to fee.
Alabama, Alabama,
We will aye be true to theel

Where the perfumed south-wind whispers,
Thy magnolia groves among,
Softer than a mother's kisses
Sweeter than a mother's song;
Where the golden jasmine trailing,
Woos the treasure laden bee,
Alabama, Alabama,
We will aye be true to thee!

Brave and pure thy men and women,
Better this than corn and wine,
Make us worthy, God in Heaven,
Of this goodly land of Thine;
Hearts as open as our doorways,
Liberal hands and spirits free,
Alabama, Alabama,
We will aye be true to thee!

Little, little, can I give thee,
Alabama, mother mine;
But that little—hand, brain, spirit,
All I have and am are thine.
Take, O take the gift and giver.
Take and serve thyself with me,
Alabama, Alabama,
I will aye be true to thee.

That was a great trip! We have traveled all over Alabama! There are a few places that we didn't have time for, though. Next time, we plan to visit the Unclaimed Baggage Center in Scottsboro. This store sells unclaimed items that were left at airports. Shoppers can find bargains on everything from books to fancy jewelry!

FAMOUS PEOPLE

Aaron, Hank (1934–), former baseball player

Carver, George Washington (1864–1943), scientist, botanist

Cole, Nat "King" (1919–1965), singer

Davis, Jefferson (1808–1889), president of the Confederate States of America

Fitzgerald, Zelda (1900–1948), author

Handy, W. C. (1873–1958), musician and composer

Harris, Emmylou (1947–), country singer

Keller, Helen (1880–1968), author and lecturer

King, Martin Luther, Jr. (1929–1968), civil rights activist and clergyman

Lee, Harper (1926–2016), author

Lewis, Carl (1961–), former track athlete

Louis, Joe (1914–1981), boxer

Mays, Willie (1931–), former baseball player

Parks, Rosa (1913–2005), civil rights activist

Red Eagle (William Weatherford) (ca. 1781–1824), Creek chief

Rice, Condoleezza (1954–), former U.S. Secretary of State

Wallace, George (1919–1998), governor

Washington, Booker T. (1856–1915), educator

Williams, Hank (1923–1953), country singer

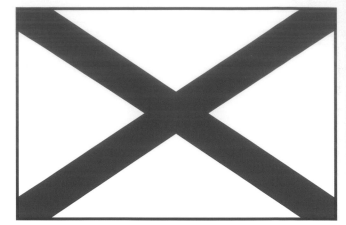

State flag

WORDS TO KNOW

bayous (BYE-ooz) shallow, slow-moving waterways

boycott (BOY-kot) a protest in which people refuse to buy or use a company's goods or services

canyon (KAN-yuhn) a deep valley where a river has worn through rock

civil rights (SIV-il RITES) the rights and freedoms of a citizen

delta (DEL-tuh) a triangle-shaped land area at the mouth of a river

economy (i-KON-uh-mee) the activities in a region that make money

gourd (GORD) the hard shell on the outside of a squash or similar plant

griffin (GRI-fuhn) a make-believe beast that's half eagle and half lion

kayak (KYE-ak) a long, narrow boat

prehistoric (pree-hi-STOR-ik) taking place before people began writing down their history

tear gas (TEER GASS) a harsh gas that stings the eyes, nose, and lungs

State seal

TO LEARN MORE

IN THE LIBRARY

Bolden, Tonya. *George Washington Carver*. New York, NY: Henry N. Abrams, 2015.

McDonough, Yona Zeldis. *Who Was Rosa Parks?* New York, NY: Grosset & Dunlap, 2010.

Ratliff, Thomas. *You Wouldn't Want to Be a Civil War Solider!* New York, NY: Scholastic 2013.

ON THE WEB

Visit our Web site for links about Alabama:

childsworld.com/links

Note to Parents, Teachers, and Librarians: We routinely verify our Web links to make sure they are safe and active sites. So encourage your readers to check them out!

PLACES TO VISIT OR CONTACT

Alabama Bureau of Tourism & Travel

alabama.travel

PO Box 4927

Montgomery, AL 36103-4927

334/242-4169

For more information about traveling in Alabama

Alabama Department of Archives and History

archives.alabama.gov

PO Box 300100

624 Washington Avenue

Montgomery, AL 36130-0100

334/242-4435

For more information about the history of Alabama

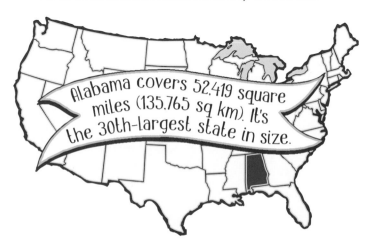

Alabama covers 52,419 square miles (135,765 sq km). It's the 30th-largest state in size.

INDEX

Bye, Heart of Dixie. We had a great time. We'll come back soon!